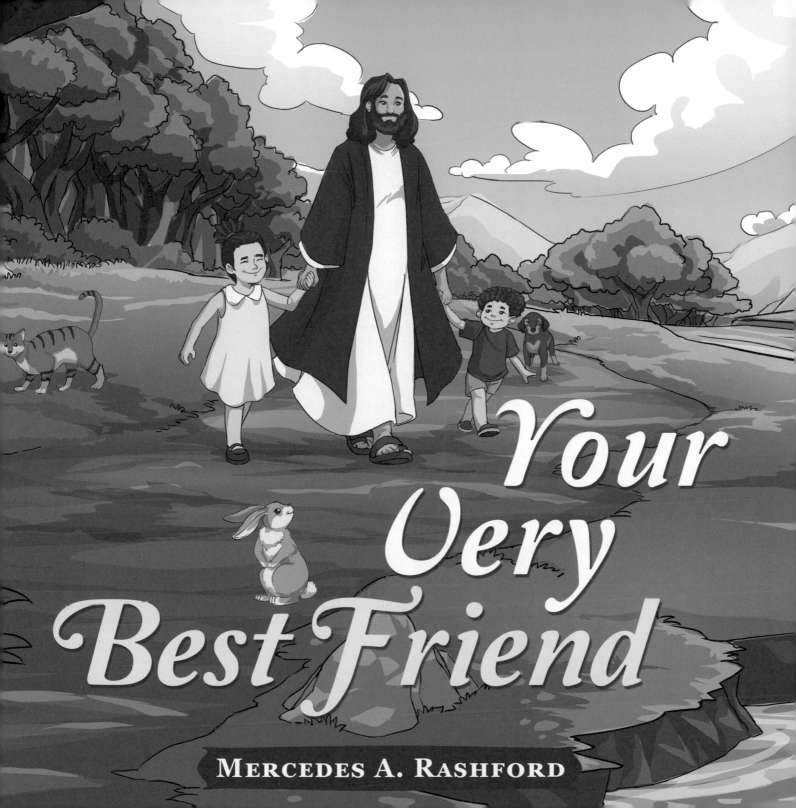

Your Very Best Friend

MERCEDES A. RASHFORD

WestBow Press books may be ordered through booksellers or by contacting:

WestBow Press
A Division of Thomas Nelson & Zondervan
1663 Liberty Drive
Bloomington, IN 47403
www.westbowpress.com
844-714-3454

ISBN: 978-1-6642-8817-1 (sc)
ISBN: 978-1-6642-8819-5 (hc)
ISBN: 978-1-6642-8818-8 (e)

Library of Congress Control Number: 2022923968

Print information available on the last page.

WestBow Press rev. date: 01/06/2023

WESTBOW
P R E S S®
A DIVISION OF THOMAS NELSON
& ZONDERVAN

Your Very Best Friend

Acknowledgments

I would like to thank Robert, my husband, who, when he heard of my desire to write this book, jumped in with both feet to make it a reality. His support gave wings to my desire. My daughter Rebekah read and edited the manuscript; my daughters Abigail and Rachel encouraged me all along the way; and my daughter Amanda and Jake, her husband, gave us the grandchildren, Ella and Ezra, who inspired this book. Finally, I would like to thank my sisters Maxine and Kathy and friend Deborah, whose confidence in me has always given me the courage to pursue what the Lord has placed on my heart. After reading my first draft, my sisters corrected thought errors and grammar and brainstormed about the best title. You all are and continue to be God's gifts to me.

To Ella, my first grandchild, who looked at me wide-eyed as I began introducing her to my very best Friend.

To Ezra, my first grandson, who is filled with life, love, and wonder.

To all my future grandchildren.

May you make Him your very best Friend throughout your whole lives, loving and depending on Him with all your heart and sharing Him with everyone you meet.

A man of many companions may come to ruin, but there is a friend who sticks closer than a brother.
Proverbs 18:24 (ESV)

Introduction

As I began telling my granddaughter about a very good Friend I would like her to meet, she looked at me so intently and with such wide eyes, hanging on to my every word, that I thought, *I had better get this right.* A few days later, the idea for this book was born.

As I tell you about my Friend,
Your hearts will skip and whirl
When you hear of His wonderful love
For you, dear boy and girl.

He was there at the beginning of time, when God, His Father, and the Holy Spirit made the world. He was there when They made the sun, the moon, and the stars.

He was with Them when They made the seas and everything in them.

He was there when God made man and woman.

He was there when the man and woman disobeyed God and sinned. Their sin separated them, and every other man and woman, from God.

Many, many years before you were born, when someone needed to come and take away the sins humans brought into the world, my Friend came as a baby.

God had to put a stop to the sin that was everywhere in the world. He couldn't be among all the men and women if they were still sinners. So, when He grew up, my friend took all the sins of the whole world onto Himself. He loves you, and everyone else too, so much that He did not want you to take the blame for your sins and be separated from God anymore.

He took your sins onto Himself by giving up His glory.

He died on a cross.

But after three days, HE ROSE TO LIFE AGAIN!
And His glory returned to Him.

He will now give His power over sin and death to you if you
simply ask Him to.

He was there when God formed you in your mommy's tummy and when you were born.

He is with you when you share and when you obey your mom and dad and grandparents. He is with you when you don't share and when you disobey them. When you disobey your parents, you separate yourself from God.

21

When my Friend died on the cross many, many years ago, you were on His mind, and if you ask Him to forgive you and take away all your sins, He will. And if You ask Him to live within your heart, He will.

And now He will be your very best Friend too.

He will always be with you, wherever you are, forever.

He will be with you while you are in school.

He will be with you while you play.

He will be with you while you are at home.

He will be with you when you are sad.

He will be with you when you are happy.

He is your best Friend, and He loves you with all His heart from now and forever.

He is your very best Friend,
Jesus.

No longer do I call you servants, for the servant does not know what his master is doing; but I have called you friends, for all that I have heard from my Father I have made known to you. John 15:15 (ESV)

Printed in the United States
by Baker & Taylor Publisher Services